James Edmund Harting

The Fauna of the Prybilov Islands

James Edmund Harting

The Fauna of the Prybilov Islands

ISBN/EAN: 9783743320611

Manufactured in Europe, USA, Canada, Australia, Japa

Cover: Foto ©ninafisch / pixelio.de

Manufactured and distributed by brebook publishing software
(www.brebook.com)

James Edmund Harting

The Fauna of the Prybilov Islands

THE FAUNA

OF THE

PRYBILOV ISLANDS

ABRIDGED FROM THE

" *Report on the Prybilov Group or Seal Islands of Alaska,*"
by HENRY W. ELLIOTT; *with an Appendix on the
Ornithology by* DR. ELLIOTT COUES (*Washington,* 1873).

BY J. E. HARTING, F.L.S. F.Z.S.

LONDON
REPRINTED FROM THE NATURAL HISTORY COLUMNS OF
"THE FIELD" FOR PRIVATE CIRCULATION
1875

LONDON:
PRINTED BY WOODFALL AND KINDER,
MILFORD LANE, STRAND, W.C.

PREFACE.

—·—

DURING the early part of 1874,* a valuable report on this remarkable group of islands, by Mr. H. W. Elliott and Dr. Elliott Coues, was published at Washington, under the auspices of the American Government. As I learn from one of the authors that only seventy-five copies of the work were issued, and as I have reason to believe that the only copy in England is the one now before me, I venture to think that a brief review of its contents (which extend over one hundred and twenty quarto pages), will be acceptable not only to naturalists, but to other readers who may be glad of some information respecting this little-known part of the world.

It will be understood that, in presenting the reader with the following remarks on the fauna of this interesting and little-known group of islands, I claim no merit on the score of originality. My notes have been either extracted from, or based upon, the observations of Mr. Elliott and Dr. Elliott Coues, to whose labours scientific naturalists are very justly indebted.

* Dr. Coues informs me that the work referred to, although dated 1873, was not actually published until either January or February, 1874.

It is to be regretted that the expensive nature and limited issue of their Report have placed the work beyond the reach of many who would otherwise, doubtless, have been glad to possess it. On this account, as well as from the interesting nature of the zoological portion of the work, I have thought that an epitome might prove acceptable to naturalists, and it seemed only due to the authors themselves that the result of their investigations should in this way, to some extent, be made more generally known.

J. E. HARTING.

24 Lincoln's Inn Fields, London.

THE FAUNA OF THE PRYBILOV
ISLANDS.

On reference to the map it will be seen that the Prybilov
Islands are situate off the coast of Alaska, in the heart, as
it were, of Behring Sea, and occupy the most isolated
position of any land in that water. The three nearest
land points, St. Mathew's Island and Nunivak, Cape
Newenham and Ounalaska, are nearly equi-distant, being
all about one hundred and eighty miles off.

Geologically speaking, the formation of these islands
(which were discovered, and named after the discoverer, by
the Russians in 1786) is recent, and in the opinion of Mr.
Elliott, who resided there during the years 1872, 1873, is
directly due to volcanic agency, which gradually upheaved
them from the sea bed. Since the period of upheaval the
sea has done much to modify and enlarge the largest
island of the group ; whilst the others, being lifted abruptly
above the power of water to carry and ice to deposit sand,
soil, and boulders, are but little changed.

St. Paul's Island, the largest of the group, must have
consisted originally of ten or twelve rocky islets or points,
upon some of which were craters sending forth breccia
and cinders, but with little or no lava overflowing. At the
present day, so thorough has been the sand-shifting, and
the grinding and lifting action of ice floes, that these
scattered islets are now bound together, as it were, by bars
of sand and boulders, which are raised above the highest

tides by wind taking the sand up from the wash of the sea, and rocks carried up there by ice fields.

The sand, which has played so important a part in the formation of St. Paul's Island, and which is almost entirely absent on and around the other islands of the group, is chiefly composed of foraminifera and diatomacea, intermixed with the volcanic base. It changes colour like a chameleon as it passes from wet to dry, being a rich steely black at the surf margin, then drying out to a soft greyish brown, succeeding to tints most delicate of reddish and pale grey when warm and drifting with the wind. Upon the sand flats and hill sides, where the sand has drifted, the most luxuriant vegetation exists.

As these sand bars were forming and gradually connecting the islets, they shut in, here and there, small bodies of sea-water, thus originating a number of pools, which have since nearly all become fresh, a most important feature for the dwellers on such inhospitable shores. These pools contain neither fish nor amphibians, but numbers of minute *rotifera* sport about at all seasons of the year when the water can be examined. A single univalve and one bivalve were the only molluscs discovered there by Mr. Elliott; but he reports that several *algæ* and water plants flourish in abundance.

The superficial area of St. Paul's Island is about thirty-three square miles, or 21,120 acres, while St. George's, the next island in point of size, has an area of about twenty-seven square miles, or 17,280 acres. Otter Island and Walrus Island are much smaller. In appearance they are described as "rough and rocky uplands, setting down boldly to the sea, or fading into wet, basaltic, mossy flats and dry sand-dune tracts."

The general elevation of these islands above the sea is not great, the highest point of St. George's being 930 feet, and of St. Paul's 600 feet.

During the months of June, July, and August the vegetation is uxulriant. Ten or twelve species of grasses—growing in every variety, from close, compact tufts to tall and isolated stems waist high—the "wild wheat" of early visitors to Alaska (*Elymus*), and above a hundred species of annuals, perennials, *Sphagnum* and other cryptogamic plants, combine to clothe the soil with a rich verdure, which contrasts pleasantly with the blue, yellow, pink, and white flowers with which it is interspersed ; while Mr. Elliott states that, on searching amongst the deep dark masses of verdure on St. Paul's Island, he has frequently found the familiar violet. The edible berries of *Empetrum nigrum* and *Rubus chamæmorus*, which ripen about the end of August and beginning of September, furnish the only fruit indigenous to the islands.

MAMMALIA.

In regard to the animal life which at certain seasons abounds upon these wild and bleak shores, the Seals, from their numbers and commercial importance, claim the largest share of attention. Four species of these sea mammals are met with, namely, the Common Seal (*Phoca vitulina*), the Fur Seal (*Callorhinus ursinus*), the Sea Lion (*Eumetopias stelleri*), and the Walrus (*Trichechus rosmarus*). The first-named is found in very small numbers at all seasons of the year, seldom more than five-and-twenty or thirty being seen at a time. They are very timid and wary, and in this respect differ greatly from the Fur Seals and Sea Lions. Mr. Elliott states that, so far as his observation goes, they are not polygamous, as the Fur Seals are, and there is no appreciable difference between the sexes. The skin is of little value compared with that of the Fur Seal, and their chief merit, says Mr. Elliott, is the greater juiciness and sweetness of their flesh to those who are partial to seal meat. The numbers in which the fur seals frequent the islands during certain months in the year are almost incredible. In the month of July, 1872, Mr. Elliott made a careful survey and computation of the fur seals both on St. Paul's Island and on St. George's Island, and by measuring the ground occupied by the different colonies (so many feet of sea margin, so many feet of average depth), and allowing so many square feet to each individual, he arrived at the astounding result of 3,030,250 seals upon the former island, and 163,420 upon the latter, making a grand total for the two islands of 3,193,670 ! These numbers, enormous as they appear, do not include, says Mr. Elliott, non-breeding seals and yearlings, which, landing in a disorderly manner, come to and from the sea at frequent and irregular intervals during the season.

On St. Paul's Island in June and July, as appears by the report, "forty-five men, in less than four working weeks, drove, killed, and skinned and salted the pelts of 72,000 seals, and doubtless could have managed 100,000 in the same time."

The mode in which these animals are driven up from the beach to the killing ground, in flocks like so many sheep, and are ultimately killed and skinned, is fully described by Mr. Elliott, and a detailed and interesting account is furnished of their reproduction, growth, and habits at all ages. This account, which is too long to be quoted here, extending over five-and-thirty quarto pages, deserves to be read *in extenso* by all who are interested in seal-life ; for, whether it be regarded from a commercial point of view or as a contribution to natural history, it is equally worthy of perusal.

Towards the second week in May the first male seals begin to approach the shore, and very grand and imposing is their appearance at this time. The sexes differ so much in size, that it is hard at first to realize their relationship. An old bull fur seal weighs over 400 lb., and measures on an average about 7 ft. in length, while the cow is only from 60 lb. to 100 lb. in weight, and about 4½ ft. in length. The old males of the herd land upon the islands about one month before the arrival of the females and young males, and on their first coming they select such positions as they consider the most eligible for their domestic requirements. These positions they hold against all comers. Naturally peaceable in their habits at other seasons, the fur seal now manifests the most pugnacious tendencies, and at the slightest indication of intrusion will plunge madly into the most frantic and sometimes the most fatal of contests. As the time approaches for the arrival of the females, these contests wax fiercer and fiercer, and the males occupying the finest places are often driven from positions they have bravely held for days, and it either happens that some stronger brute kills the tenant of the ground he covets, or drives him further inland, where he has to run the gauntlet of all the back rows. The ladies also greatly prefer the front seats, and, although they seemingly are passive endurers of whatever fate may attend them, they greatly resent being sent back to the outer circles. As they approach the shore, they have a first anxiety which seemingly makes them indifferent to their reception, and the males nearest to the sea margin select as they arrive such beauties as may strike their ardent fancy. These they endeavour to snatch at and carry off, hoping to add beauty after beauty until their harem is complete ; but this selection is not a matter of undisturbed enjoyment. Far from it ; the bitter jealousy of surrounding neighbours impels them to dispute every fresh acquisition, and the chances are that, while some stout old bull is contesting tooth and nail for the latest capture he is endeavouring at the risk of his life to secure, some other in the rear is quietly appropriating the choicest of his wives, who has already commenced to make herself comfortable in her new home.

In a few hours after landing the young of the year are born—single, almost helpless, little black objects, with great staring eyes, and restless bodies, capable of enduring hunger for nine days (as has been proved by cruel experiment) ; but they soon grow active and intelligent, and after a month or two spent in the enjoyment of the society of little colonies of pups of like age, and with no distinguishable difference in shape or individual characteristics, they make their way to the water, but it is only after frequent trials and many helpless failures that the young seal acquires its sea-going qualities. The noise made by thousands of the animals is incessant. They have natuially an evil smell, and as a large percentage lose their lives in the frequent conflicts waged amongst the males, and numbers of the young die off from neglect, cruelty, and disease incidental to all young animals, a dreadful stench is soon created; and, although there is a kind of system in the arrangement of these colonies, the sanitary measures are, to say the least, not perfect.

The most strange fact recorded by the officials is to the effect that the old seals never return to the sea from the time of their first arrival, when they are huge masses of fat, until the close of the season, when they drag down their exhausted bodies once more to the refreshing deep; and during all these months, from May to August, they taste no food or water; yet they are active, full of fire and irritability, proud of their large families, and ever watchful of their young ones. Some old bulls have from ten to fifteen wives each, although there are cases on record where a little colony of forty-five females were guarded against all intrusion by some lusty old male, while in the back rows four or five wives were seen to spend a miserable existence, cut off from the larger societies of their sex.

As the year advances, the fur seal sheds his outer coat which is coarse and hair-like, as well as his under coat of fine fur. Soon after this the winter coat begins to appear, and in a very short time the fine fur is perfect. Then it is that the hunters, who have frequently visited the various colonies in their rounds of inspection, without disturbing the various families by walking amongst them, begin to make their arrangements for capturing the young males. These young males reside in small groups near the water line, and at the least alarm are prepared to escape into the sea. It is necessary, therefore, for the hunters to creep in single file along the margin of the sea without attracting observation, and at a given signal to rise up suddenly and, with loud shouts and frantic gesticulations, to force the seals to turn their heads inland. Like frightened sheep they crowd into a flock, and then begins the long journey overland to the slaughtering places. In the herd, as it is driven along, are many old ones, whose skins would be of no use, and sometimes these, turning to contest the right of their captors, get left behind, or, struggling along with their less bulky fellow-captives, sink down from exhaustion and die where they halt. The remainder, driven over the sandy flats and gentle elevations, arrive in due time at the " killing grounds ; " where a further selection is made, and those only are killed whose skins are of marketable value. The skins are quickly torn off, and being roughly salted, are tied with others into bundles, for shipment to England. The bodies, rich in costly seal oil, and laden with offensive flesh, are left to pollute the already foul air of the island, at no great distance from the dwellings of the colonists.

All the fur seal skins come to London to be dressed, and, as the process is a very tedious and expensive one, occupying at least two months in the preparation, the original value of from twenty to thirty shillings for a salted skin soon increases, after it has been plucked by some secret process and is ready for the furrier, to the value of from three to eight pounds sterling for each skin, according to its beauty and fine texture.

The Sea Lion (*Eumetopias stelleri*), although frequenting the islands in large droves in the breeding season, is not nearly so numerous as the fur seal. Mr. Elliott roughly estimated their numbers at from thirty to thirty-five thousand on St. Paul's and contiguous islets, and not more than seven or eight thousand on St. George's. This species is highly appreciated by the natives for the superior quality of the flesh ; for the hides, which make excellent skin-boats ; for the intestines, out of which waterproof coats are manufactured ; and for the skin of

the flippers, which, being tough and elastic, makes service-
able soles for boots.

The Walrus of Behring Sea, which Mr. Elliott considers
perfectly distinct from the walrus of the North Atlantic
and Greenland, is at the present time only to be seen on
Walrus Island, these animals being so shy and timid that
they have deserted the other islands as they became
populated by man. They are of but little commercial
value, their ivory being of poor quality, porous, pithy, and
yellow, while the oil is of low grade, and the hide worth-
less. An adult male averages about 12 ft. in length and
10 ft. or 12 ft. in girth ; but one old bull shot by the
natives on Walrus Island in July, 1872, was nearly 13 ft.
long, with the enormous girth of 14 ft.

So important and valuable is the Alaska seal trade that,
in order to prevent the extermination of these animals
upon the islands (which are leased by the American
Government to the Alaska Commercial Company), an Act
of Congress was passed in 1870 making it illegal to kill
seals in any other months than June, July, September, and
October, expressly prohibiting at all times their destruc-
tion by firearms, and limiting the number to be killed per
annum. The wisdom of such a precautionary measure is in-
contestable. Mr. Elliott, who states that "the Government
interests on these islands represent the commercial value
of twenty or twenty-five millions of dollars at least," be-
lieves that no legislation has ever done more to improve the
condition of any people than the Act of Congress has which
set aside the Prybilov Islands and their inhabitants from the
territory of Alaska, as a Government reservation, leasing
them to the Alaska Commercial Company in July, 1870.

The truth of this will be evident to any one who contrasts the present condition of the inhabitants with what
it was previously to the granting of the lease. These
people, of every nationality, now so well and comfortably
clad, were at the time of the transfer so poor and badly
provided for that in many instances they could scarcely
cover their nakedness. Under Russian rule they existed

in absolute squalor, but are now living in snug houses, and are in receipt of good wages from the company.

Only a small proportion of the present population are descendants of the pioneers who were brought by the Russian-American Company to the islands in 1786–87—a colony of one hundred and thirty-seven souls, organized at Sitka, and principally recruited from the Aleuts at Ounalaska.

The manners and customs of these people possess in themselves nothing of a barbarous character. Having lived so long under and with the Russians, they have adopted many of their customs, and, according to Mr. Elliott, have many commendable traits in the composition of their character.

The population of St. Paul's Island is about two hundred and forty men, women, and children ; and of St. George one hundred and twenty. It has neither increased nor diminished for the last fifty years, but would have fallen off had not recruits been regularly drawn from the mainland and other islands, the births not being equal to the deaths. But in view of the great improvement in their condition, says Mr. Elliott, it may be reasonably anticipated that these people will at least hold their own, even though they do not increase to any noteworthy degree.

These remarks upon the islanders may seem to be, and indeed are, in the nature of a digression from my theme ; but when it is remembered that by far the most important feature in the fauna of these islands is the seal-life which abounds there, it will be conceded that some notice of the sealers could scarcely be dispensed with.

Turning from a consideration of the seals and sea lions which, as we have seen, abound at certain seasons upon these islands, the few small mammalia which exist, whether indigenous, introduced, or carried thither on the ice, may be briefly enumerated.

Sea otters—which at one time were numerous, and which apparently suggested a name for one of the islands, Otter Island—have long since become extinct. Bishop

Veniaminov, in the only Russian treatise upon these islands which exists, and which Mr. Elliott has translated in the work under notice, speaks of them as affording ornamental fur to the early settlers, and states that in 1811 they were nearly extinct, and within the next thirty years became entirely so. His observations were published in 1840.

Sometimes the ice brought over bears and red foxes ; but they were never allowed to live. The latter were especially destroyed, as it was feared that they might spoil the breed already existing in regard to the colour of the fur. At the present time blue and white cross foxes (*Vulpes lagopus*) find a comfortable retreat amongst the numerous chinks and crevices in the basaltic formation, and keep themselves in good condition by feeding upon young seals, birds, and eggs in the summer, and in winter upon the dead bodies of the seals left upon the killing grounds. Mr. Elliott was much struck by their temerity (on St. George's Island especially) in climbing up and down the faces of almost inaccessible cliffs seeking eggs. They go, at a full run or in a stealthy tread, over the brows of cliffs that fairly overhang the sea six and nine hundred feet below. They always bring the eggs up in their mouths, and carry them back from the brink of the precipice, where they leisurely suck them, usually biting the shell out at the larger end. The guillemots suffer most from these marauders, the only natural foes with which the birds on these islands have to contend.

The only other indigenous mammal is a small lemming (*Myodes obensis*), which is restricted, singularly enough, to the Island of St. George, where it is exceedingly abundant, burrowing in all directions under and among the grassy hummocks above the sea margin.

The islands have hitherto escaped from any visitation of rats ; but mice have been brought from the ships, and are great pests in winter. Mr. Elliott reports that stock cannot be profitably raised, on account of the severe winters, at which season, and for several months, they

would require so much food and shelter as to entail a
very considerable expense—grain having to come from
San Francisco, and the dampness of the summer season
rendering hay-growing impracticable. Mr. Elliott is
inclined to think that, although cattle could not thrive
there, reindeer might be introduced with success, and
would afford a supply, both in summer and winter, of
good fresh meat.

AVES.

An account of the birds which periodically resort
to the islands in countless thousands has been made the
subject of an " Appendix " to the " Report " now under
notice, and the fact that this " Appendix " has been prepared by Dr. Elliott Coues is of itself a sufficient recom-
mendation to the notice of ornithologists.

The list of species is not large, amounting only to forty,
including all the migrants and accidental visitants, while
the number of species which breed upon the islands is
limited to about a dozen. It is, however, the multitude
of individuals, and not of species, which strikes the visitor
who beholds them with wonderment akin to awe. The
spectacle of birds nesting on St. George's Island in
thousands, crowding a line of sea cliffs twenty miles in
extent, is a sight of extreme novelty and interest, affording the naturalist opportunity for observation and investi-
gation into the most minute details of the reproduction
of these vast flocks of circumboreal waterfowl. St. Paul's
Island, owing to the low character of its shore line—a
large portion of which is but slightly elevated above the
sea, and sandy—is not visited by such myriads as are
seen at St. George ; but the small rock known as Walrus
Island, is fairly covered with sea birds, while the Otter
Island bluffs are crowded to their utmost capacity.

The species which chiefly compose these large flocks on
St. George's Island are guillemots, or " arries " as they are
locally termed (*Lomvia californica* and *Lomvia arra*), two

species of kittiwake (*Larus tridactylus* and *Larus brevi-rostris*) and little horned puffins, or "chooch-kies" as the natives call them (*Simorhynchus microceros*) ; while on Walrus Island are found the glaucous gull (*Larus glaucus*), red-legged kittiwake (*Larus brevirostris*), two species of puffin (*Fratercula corniculata* and *cirrhata*), and the red-faced cormorant (*Graculus bicristatus*).

The excellent account which Dr. Elliott Coues has given of these and other species met with on the islands is too long to be quoted entire ; but, omitting all descriptions, and epitomizing his remarks, many of which are extremely interesting, the species are detailed as follows :—

TURDUS MIGRATORIUS (Linn.).—The American Robin was seen by Mr. Elliott on St. Paul's Island in October, 1872. The natives recognized it as a casual visitant.

ANORTHURA ALASCENSIS (Coues).—The Alaskan Winter Wren, which is larger and darker than the ordinary North American species, and has a much longer and stouter bill, is a permanent resident on St. George's Island, but has not been met with on St. Paul's, although distant but twenty-seven miles to the north-west. Its nest is built in small deep holes and crevices in the cliffs, and is composed of soft dry grass and feathers, roofed over, with an entrance at the side. It is said to lay eight or ten eggs. In the nesting season the male bird is very lively, flying incessantly from plant to plant, or rock to rock, singing a shrill and loud song, and making a great noise for such a small bird. In this respect it resembles the common wren of Europe. Mr. Dall found it resident and abundant on the rocky cliffs of Amaknak Island, Ounalaska. The native name, "limmer-shin," says Mr. Elliott, signifies a chew of tobacco, and is given on account of the resemblance of this wee bird in size and colour to a tobacco quid.

LEUCOSTICTE TEPHROCOTIS (Brandt).—The Grey-eared Finch. The Alaskan form or variety of this species has been described by Professor Baird as *Leucosticte littoralis*, and by Dr. Coues as *L. griseinucha ;* but the latter naturalist, from a subsequent examination of numerous intermediate forms, now considers that, although much larger than the typical *tephrocotis*, and otherwise different in the *pictura* of the head, he is unable to separate it specifically, considering both forms, *littoralis* and *griseinucha*, as the single Arctic representative of *tephrocotis* proper. The bird is resident on the islands, and is particularly common on St. George's, feeding on various seeds and insects, as well as on the larvæ which swarm on the killing grounds of the sealers. It consorts in pairs throughout the year, never going in flocks, and seldom flying or feeding alone. It has no song, but utters a low mellow chirp. The nest is neatly made of dry grass and moss, thick, and compactly woven, placed on the faces of the basaltic and breccia cliffs which rise from the shore-line of the islands. The eggs are white, suffused, when fresh, with a delicate rosy blush. The birds, which are fearless and confiding, flutter in the most familiar manner round the village huts. In the summer of 1873 a pair built their nest and reared a brood under the eaves of the old Greek church at St. George's.

PLECTROPHANES NIVALIS (Linn.).—The Snow Bunting, or Snow Bird, is another permanent resident on the islands, but, unlike the last-named, is somewhat shy and retiring, nesting high on the rocky broken uplands, and only entering the villages during unusually severe or protracted cold weather. It builds an elegant nest of soft dry grass, and lines it warmly with a thick bed of feathers, placing it on the ground generally beneath some lava-slate, or at the foot of a boulder. The eggs, usually five in number, are described by Dr. Coues, but are now well known in collections.

PLECTROPHANES LAPPONICA (Linn.).—The Lapland Bunting, or Longspur, a resident bird, is a delightful vocalist, singing all through the month of June in the most charming manner, rising high in the air, and hovering on fluttering wings over its sitting mate. The song is only too short, lasting but a few moments, though continually repeated. The bird is much shyer than the Snow Bunting, rarely entering the village. It is most abundant on St. Paul's, where, unlike the last-named species, it seeks the low grassy grounds, both for food and nesting, being never found among the rough boulders which are frequented by the snow bunting. The eggs, usually five in number, are extremely variable in colour, but are now too well known to require description.

CORVUS CORAX (Linn.).—The Raven, though not indigenous, has a claim to notice in the present list from the attempt which has been made to introduce and acclimatize it. The Russians tried the experiment of bringing up from Sitka and Ounalaska a number of Ravens, with the view of inducing them to live and breed upon the islands, where they would be most invaluable as scavengers ; but the birds invariably, sooner or later, took flight for the Aleutian Islands or the mainland. The natives state that the experiment has failed in consequence of the individuals introduced being old birds, and consider that if young birds were brought over and liberated they would remain, and probably breed there.

FALCO SACER (Forster).—Under this title Dr. Coues has referred to an immature specimen of one of the large northern falcons, presumably the Greenland Falcon, which was obtained on St. Paul's in March, 1873. In his " Key to North American Birds," p. 213, Dr. Coues has treated *Falco candicans, islandicus,* and *gyrfalco* (which are usually regarded as distinct species) as mere varieties of one species, which he identifies with *Falco sacer* of Forster (Phil. Trans. lxxii., p. 423, 1772), an opinion which has probably taken many European ornithologists by surprise. It is, accordingly, not quite clear what the Prybilov bird was, especially as no description of it is supplied.

Hawks, as well as Owls, are stated to be occasionally seen on the islands, the latter more especially in winter, but no species of either has been determined for certain. Dr. Coues thinks that the Hawk Owl (*Surnia ulula*) probably occurs there.

Amongst the waders and wildfowl met with on these bleak inhospitable shores, the following are included in Mr. Elliott's list :—

CHARADRIUS FULVUS (Gmelin).—A few Golden Plovers land on the Prybilov Islands in April, or early in May, on their way north to breed, but never remain long. They return in greater number in the latter part of September, and grow fat upon the larvæ generated on the ground where the seals are killed, leaving for the south by the end of October. It is worthy of note that the only specimen preserved by Mr. Elliott, and which was obtained on St. Paul's Island on May 2, 1873, has been determined to be the Asiatic *fulvus*, and not the American *virginicus*. Referring to this specimen, Dr. Coues says: "We have made the comparison with numerous examples before us from various Asiatic and Pacific localities, finding the present specimen indistinguishable [from them]. Length about 9·50 ; wing, 6·40 ; tail, 2·60 ; tarsus, 1·60 ; middle toe and claw, 1·1 ; culmen, ·95. There is a yellowish suffusion about the head, particularly along the superciliary line, which is hardly to be noticed in the ordinary North American bird."

STREPSILAS INTERPRES (Linn.).—The Turnstone, according to Mr. Elliott, arrives upon the Prybilov Islands in flocks of thousands about the third week in July, and takes its departure about the 10th of September. It does not breed there. On its arrival it is quite poor in flesh, but, feeding upon the larvæ and maggots which are generated upon the killing grounds of the sealers, it rapidly improves in condition, and becomes excessively fat, so much so, indeed, that a bird shot on the wing often bursts open on falling to the ground.

Dr. Elliott Coues states that numerous specimens of Turnstones shot on these islands all indicated an interesting approach to the peculiar features of the North-west American form, *melanocephalus*, in the extent and intensity of the black area on the head, neck, and back, the chestnut colouring being reduced mainly to a scapular patch, some edging of the feathers of the interscapular region, and a diffuse area on the wing coverts. "The upper parts of the body are otherwise black, relieved by the broad pure white

area of the lower back and rump, and varied with white
on the crown and cervix. The front, sides of head and neck,
throat, and entire breast, are intense black, relieved by
loral, gular, auricular, and latero-cervical white areas." It
is clear from this description that the species was *S.
interpres*, and not *melanocephalus*, which never has any
trace of chestnut colour in the plumage, and which invariably has a black chin. It is also clear that Dr. Coues'
description applies to birds of the year, and adults which
have partially cast off their summer plumage ; and this is
further evidenced by the season of the year at which the
specimens were obtained. It does not appear that these
birds visit the islands during the spring migration ; but,
were specimens procurable there at that season, a much
more remarkable contrast of colour would be observable
on comparison with specimens of *melanocephalus*. It seems
to me that the latter form is fully entitled to rank as a
species, instead of as a variety merely of *interpres*, as
opined by Dr. Coues. Referring to the Prybilov species,
Mr. Elliott states that he met with it at sea, 800 miles from
the nearest land, flying north-west towards the Aleutian
Islands.

LOBIPES HYPERBOREUS (Linn.).—A few stray pairs of
this Phalarope breed upon the Prybilov Islands, nesting
around the margins of the fresh-water pools. Mr. Elliott
has described the young, which he found there, as being
only two or three inches long, with the bill about a third
of an inch in length, and no thicker than an ordinary
dressing-pin. The down of the head, neck, and upper
parts is rich brownish yellow, variegated with brownish
black, the crown being of this colour mixed with yellow,
and a long stripe extends down the back, flanked with
one over each hip, another across the rump, and a shoulder
spot on each side. The under parts are greyish silvery
white. The old bird when startled, or solicitous for the
safety of its brood, utters a succession of sonorous " tweet "
sounds, quickly repeated, with long intervals of silence.

PHALAROPUS FULICARIUS (Linn.).—Although much

more abundant at times than the preceding species, this Phalarope does not breed on the Prybilov Islands. It is found, like the other, by the marshy margins of pools, solitary or paired, but never in flocks. The earliest arrivals occur in June, but the birds reappear in greatest numbers about the 15th of August. They all leave by the 5th of October.

TRINGA PTILOCNEMIS, Coues.—Under this name Dr. Coues has described a new species of Sandpiper which Mr. Elliott discovered on the Prybilov Islands, and which breeds there in some numbers. It is intermediate in size between *Tringa crassirostris* (Temm. and Schleg.) and the well-known Dunlin, *Tringa alpina* (Linn.), and is similarly coloured, assuming, as both these species do, a black breast in the breeding season, and a more or less rufous coloration of the dorsal plumage ; the under parts becoming pure white in the winter, and the upper parts, at the same season, almost uniformly grey. Dr. Coues describes an adult bird in breeding plumage, " With somewhat the general appearance of *Tringa alpina*, but the black area on the under parts pectoral, not abdominal. Bill about as long as the head, straight to the end,* compressed, stout, and high at the base, with very long nasal fossæ, reaching to within ⅛th inch of the tip, and deep at the base ; the groove of the under mandible co-extensive in length, but linear throughout. Feathers on side of under mandible extending beyond those on the upper; the interramal feathers projecting still a little way further. Legs very short (much as in *Tringa maritima*) ; tibial feathers reaching nearly or quite to the suffrago ; tarsus shorter than the bill, or than the middle toe and claw. Wings and tail as usual throughout the genus." In a foot-note Dr. Coues adds, " It may appropriately be named *T. ptilocnemis* in allusion to the feathered tibiæ." He considers it most nearly allied to *Tringa maritima.* Minute details of the adult plumage

* Dr. Coues admits, however, in a foot-note, that " in other specimens, and usually, the bill is considerably longer, exceeding the head, and decidedly decurved at the end."

are added, and a description given of the newly hatched young, taken early in July, and the nearly fledged, not quite grown young, taken late in July. The measurements, according to Dr. Coues, are : " Length apparently about 9·50 inches ; wing, about ·5 ; tail, 2·50 ; bill, 1·10 to 1·40 ; tarsus, ·9 to 1 ; middle toe and claw 1·05 to 1·20." "The sexes," he says, " are not distinguishable by any outward mark." Professor Baird was kind enough to forward me one of Mr. Elliott's specimens, from St. Paul's Island, and, from its large size and characteristic markings, I at first mistook it for a small example of *Tringa crassirostris ;* but subsequently, on instituting a careful comparison, I found that it was quite distinct from this species, and I accordingly described it as new (Proc. Zool. Soc., 1874, p. 242), naming it TRINGA GRACILIS, and figured the bill, foot, and contour of the tail feathers, as compared with those of *Tringa crassirostris* and *T. alpina*, to illustrate the most distinctive characters of the species.

My remarks on the subject were as follows :—

" Through the kindness of Professor Spencer Baird, I received some months ago a specimen of a Sandpiper from St. Paul's Island, Alaska, with a request that I would examine and report upon it. It resembled at first sight a very large Dunlin (*Tringa alpina*), in partial summer plumage, and with the breast more or less spotted with black ; but its superior size showed at once that it could not belong to that species. The only other *Tringa* at all resembling it with which I was then acquainted being *Tringa crassirostris.* of Temminck and Schlegel, from China, Japan, the Malay countries, and Australia, I hastily but erroneously came to the conclusion that it should be referred to that species ; and without waiting to institute any comparison of specimens, I wrote to Professor Baird accordingly. This was unfortunate ; for on subsequently making a more careful examination, and comparing the bird in question with specimens in my collection of both *T. alpina* and *T. crassirostris*, I found to my surprise

that it differed materially from both, being much smaller
than *T. crassirostris* although considerably larger than
T. alpina, and in several other respects, as I shall pre-
sently point out, holding an intermediate position between
these two species. I have now no hesitation in saying that
it may be regarded as a new and hitherto undescribed
bird, and I accordingly propose to name it *Tringa gracilis*.

" It may be described as follows :—

" TRINGA GRACILIS, sp. nov.

" *T. similis* alpinæ *sed conspicue major. Notæi plumis*
nigris, late rufo-marginatis ; pilco fuscescente, rufo
nigroque striolato ; capitis et colli lateribus dilute rufes-
centibus, maculis minutis fuscis ; uropygio nigro ;
gula et fronte albis ; macula pectorali magna nigra ;
abdomine crissoque albis ; tectricibus alarum pallide
fuscis, albido limbatis ; remigibus fuscis, scapis pure
albis ; subalaribus albis ; rectricibus lateralibus pallide
fuscis, albolimbatis ; rostro et pedibus nigricantibus.
(*Ptil. æstiv.*) *Long. tot.* 10 *poll., rostr.* 1·5, *alæ* 5·5,
tars. 1, *dig. med. cum ung.* 1·1.
" *Hab.* St. Paul's Island, Alaska.

" The specimen from which the above description is taken
was most kindly presented to me by Professor Baird, with
the information that it had been obtained with several
others on the island above mentioned in the month of
July, 1872. It is evidently in summer plumage ; and
being at this season black-breasted, like the Dunlin
(*Tringa alpina*), we may fairly assume that in winter, like
that species, it loses all trace of black upon the breast,
and has the whole of the under parts pure white. The
same has been ascertained to be the case with *Tringa*
crassirostris.
" In order to give a better idea of the size of this new
Sandpiper, I subjoin the following measurements of bill,
wing, tarsus, and middle toe, as compared with the same

parts in the two better-known species to which it is allied :—

	Entire length. in.	Bill. in.	Wing. in.	Tars. in.	Mid. toe. in.
T. crassirostris	11	1·7	7	1·4	1·2
T. gracilis .	10	1·5	5·5	1	1·1
T. alpina .	8	1·4	4·5	1	0·9

" In *T. crassirostris* (Plate, fig. 7) the bill is unusually deep at the base, and laterally much compressed ; the wings long, with broad and powerful flight-feathers ; the tail (fig. 9) almost square ; the tibia for some portion of its length bare ; the tarsus (fig. 8) longer than the middle toe ; the toes comparatively short, stout, and well margined, as in *Tringa canutus*,* while the nails are long and curved.

"In *T. gracilis*, as in *T. alpina* (see Plate), the bill (fig. 4) is more slender and less compressed at the sides ; the wings, though long, have narrower and more feeble flight-feathers ; the central feathers of the tail (fig. 6) are prolonged beyond the rest ; the tibia is feathered nearly to the tarsal joint ; and the tarsus is somewhat shorter than the middle toe and nail. The toes (fig. 5) are thus comparatively longer, and, besides being more slender, are not margined to the same extent as in *T. crassirostris*, although this feature is more noticeable in *T. gracilis* than in *T. alpina*, which may be said to be almost devoid of any emargination, while the nails are shorter and weaker.

"A considerable difference is observable in the contour of the tail in these three species, as may be seen from the accompanying figures (Plate, figs. 3, 6, 9).

"In the letter which accompanied the specimen now

"* Many naturalists who have met with *T. crassirostris* for the first time as Messrs. Hume, Swinhoe, Blakiston, and others, have likened it, from its robust size, to the Knot (*T. canutus*) ; and Mr. Swinhoe has named it the Chinese Knot. There can be little doubt, however, from the character of its seasonal changes of plumage, as well as from certain similarities of structure, that its affinities are with the Dunlin (*T. alpina*).

before me, Professor Baird likened the species to *Tringa maritima*, but remarked that he had received 'specimens in which the black pectoral spot is much more distinct and better defined' [than in the specimen he sent me], 're-sembling somewhat that of *T. alpina*, only situated con-siderably further up on the breast.' In some respects no doubt the bird in question does resemble *T. maritima*, as, for instance, in having the tibia more or less feathered, in having the tarsus if anything shorter than the middle toe, and again in the contour of the tail. But it differs entirely from *T. maritima* in the character of the nuptial plumage, as also in the colour of the soft parts—the legs and toes in *T. maritima*, as also the base of the mandibles, being of a yellowish clay colour, while the same parts in *T. gracilis*, as in *T. alpina*, are black.

" The discovery of this new species of sandpiper will be as gratifying to ornithologists as it was unexpected, and I feel much indebted to Professor Baird for having afforded me an opportunity of bringing it to their notice. Although it has only been met with hitherto upon St. Paul's Island, Alaska, there is no reason to suppose that it has a very restricted range. On the contrary, being capable, like all its congeners, of powerful flight, I should at least expect to hear of it on the mainland on both sides of Behring Sea, and probably as as far northward as the Arctic Circle.

" Moreover, it is not unlikely that on the west coast of North America it may have been mistaken for *Tringa alpina*, var. *americana*, Cassin. It should be observed that in comparing the dimensions of the species above named, I have preferred to take an average specimen of *T. alpina* without reference to locality (it happens to have been obtained in England), rather than select, as I might have done, an American example, which would only differ in having the bill equal to, or slightly longer than, that of *T. gracilis ;* for this long-billed variety, as I have before pointed out (P. Z. S. 1871, p. 115), is not confined to the American continent.

" PS. (June 20, 1874).—Since the foregoing remarks were written, I have been in correspondence with Dr. Elliott Coues on the subject of a *Tringa* recently described by him as *Tringa ptilocnemis* in an 'Appendix' to Mr. H. W. Elliott's 'Report on the Prybilov Islands.' This 'Appendix' I have not yet seen, although Dr. Coues has most kindly forwarded proof-sheets of the body of the work ; but I have no doubt, from his letters to me on the subject, that his bird is the species now under notice."

I had not then seen the excellent description of this bird given by Dr. Elliott Coues in the Appendix to the Report now before me, or I should have been glad to have availed myself of the interesting account which he has there supplied of its various changes of plumage and of its nesting.

According to the observations of Mr. Elliott, this is the only wader which breeds on the Prybilov Islands, with the exception of a stray couple now and then of *Phalaropus hyperboreus*. It makes its appearance early in May, and repairs to the dry uplands and mossy hummocks, where it breeds. The nest is formed by the selection of a particular mossy bunch, upon which the bird sits until a depression is made large enough to contain the eggs. These are four in number, and pyriform in shape, measuring 1·55 in. by 1·08 in., and resemble those of the Purple Sandpiper (*Tringa maritima*.) The ground is nearly clay colour, but with an appreciable olivaceous shade ; the markings are large, bold, and numerous, of rich burnt-umber brown, of varying depth according to the quantity of the pigment. These surface markings occur all over the shell, except the extreme point, and are solidly massed by confluence on the larger half of the egg ; all the markings are strong, as if laid on freely with a heavily-charged brush. With these surface spots occur numerous shell markings of the same character, but of course obscure, presenting a stone-grey or purplish grey shade ; some of them look as if the colour of the surface spots had " run," and soaked into the olivaceous drab of

the general surface. A nest containing the full comple-
ment of four eggs was taken by Mr. Elliott on the 19th
June, 1873, on St. George's Island. The eggs at that date
were quite fresh. Others were found to hatch out within
twenty days. The young come from the shell in a thick
yellowish down, with dark brown markings on the head
and back, getting the plumage of their parents and taking
to wing as early as the 10th of August ; and at this season
old and young flock together for the first time, and confine
themselves to the sand beaches and surf margins about the
islands for a few weeks, when they take flight during the
first week of September, and disappear until the opening
of the new season.

The parent bird is most fearless and devoted to its
young, and will flutter by the hour around the intruder
who approaches the nest, uttering a low, piping note. It
also makes a sound exactly like a tree-frog, and, until Mr.
Elliott had traced the sound to its source, he searched
several weeks unavailingly for the reptile, misled by the
call of the bird.

LIMOSA UROPYGIALIS (Gould).—This well-known Old-
world species is the only Godwit found upon the Prybilov
Islands. It is but migratory, however, and does not breed
there. It comes in a straggling manner early in May,
passing northward with little delay, and reappears towards
the end of August in flocks of a dozen to fifty.

Mr. Dall obtained two eggs on June 18, 1868, at Kutlik,
Alaska. These differ as much from each other as eggs of
this species do from those of other species. The ground
colour of one is greenish olive, of the other pale olive-grey.
In the former the markings are all subdued neutral tints,
apparently in the shell ; in the latter the markings are
nearly all on the surface, and quite bright chocolate brown.
In both cases the markings are numerous and of inde-
terminate shape, mostly small, and generally distributed,
though tending to aggregate at the larger end, where
alone they lose their distinctness in coalescing to form a
splashed area.

HETEROSCELUS INCANUS (Gmelin).—This large and widely distributed Sandpiper visits the Prybilov Islands regularly as a migrant, but does not remain to breed there. It arrives early in June, and subsequently reappears towards the end of July, when it may be found on the rocky beaches. It never visits the uplands, and is a very shy and quiet bird.

NUMENIUS BOREALIS (Forster).—This Curlew occurs as a rare visitant to the Prybilov Islands. A solitary specimen was obtained, on St. Paul's, by Mr. Elliott, in June, 1872. It breeds apparently in great numbers in the Anderson River region, whence a large series of eggs was forwarded by Mr. R. Macfarlane to the Smithsonian Institution. The nest is placed in a depression on the barren plain, and formed of decayed leaves. The eggs, four in number, are usually all laid by the third week in June. They vary much in colour, the ground being olive drab, tending either to green, grey, or brown, as the case may be, and the markings, which are bold and numerous, dark chocolate, bistre, and sepia brown of different depths, with the usual stone-grey shell markings. These always tend to aggregation at the larger end, or at least are more numerous on the major half of the egg, though the distribution is sometimes nearly uniform, and in no instance is the small end entirely free from spots. An average-sized egg measures 2in. by 1·45 in.

ANSER CANAGICA (Sevast).—The Emperor Goose, or Painted Goose as it is also called, visits the islands only as a straggler, sometimes landing in so exhausted a state that the natives capture a whole flock in open chase over the grass, the birds being unable to use their wings for flight. Mr. Elliott states that he found the flesh of this bird, contrary to report, free from any unpleasant flavour, and, in fact, very good. The objectionable quality is only skin deep, and may be got rid of by due care in the preparation of the bird for the table. Mr. Dall found this fine goose abundant in the Kuselrak Slough, at the mouth of the Yukon, where it breeds.

ANSER CANADENSIS (Pallas) occasionally straggles to

the islands in small squads of ten to thirty, evidently driven by high winds from their customary line of migration along the mainland. Though not breeding here, it occasionally spends weeks at a time on the lakelets and uplands before taking flight either north or south, as the season may be.

Dr. Elliott Coues thinks there is no doubt that the so-called *Anser leucoparcia* is nothing more than a race of the common *canadensis*. The supposed specific characters, he says, are not constant.

ANAS BOSCHAS (Linn.).—The common Wild Duck, although not a regular visitor to the Prybilov group, has occasionally been noted there. During the nesting season of 1872, a pair bred on Polavina Lakelet, St. Paul's Island, and several were observed later in the fall. The mallard has also been met with on St. George's Island.

MARECA PENELOPE (Linn.).—It is an interesting fact that the Widgeon which visits the Prybilov Islands is not *M. americana*, as might have been anticipated, but the true *M. penelope*, as Mr. Elliott's specimens attest. It is but seldom seen, however; never in pairs, does not breed on the islands, and apparently the few individuals noted during Mr. Elliott's two years' observations were weather-bound or astray.

HARELDA GLACIALIS (Linn.).—The Long-tailed Duck is common and resident. It breeds on the akelets and sloughs of St. Paul's in limited numbers. It is a very noisy bird, particularly in the spring, when, on the breaking up of the ice it comes into the open reaches of water, with its peculiar, sonorous, and reiterated cry, which rings cheerfully upon the ear after the silence and desolation of an ice-bound Arctic winter.

HISTRIONICUS TORQUATUS (Linn.).—The Harlequin Duck is common on and around the island shores, floating idly amid the surf in flocks of fifty or sixty, or basking and preening on the beaches and outlying rocks. It may be seen all the year round, excepting only when forced away by the ice floes. Although Mr. Elliott is confident that it

breeds on the islands, he did not succeed in finding the
nest, nor could he learn that the eggs were known to the
natives. His experience of the bird differs somewhat from
that of Mr. Dall, who states (Trans. Chicago Acad. i., p. 298)
that is " essentially a solitary species, found alone or in
pairs only in the most retired spots, on the small rivers
flowing into the Yukon, where it breeds."   Mr. Elliott did
not find it particularly wild or shy, and numbers are killed
by the natives every fall and spring.   It is a remarkably
silent bird ; Mr. Elliott never heard it utter any cry.   It is
gregarious, and the females seem to outnumber the males
in the proportion of two to one.

SOMATERIA STELLERI (Pallas).—A few of Steller's
Eider were observed, but not secured, on St. Paul's in the
spring of 1812 (?).   Two were shot at the East Point, St.
George's, the same year, but it can only be regarded as a
rare straggler to these islands.   Dr. Coues considers that
in all essential respects this duck is a true eider.

From the situation and character of these remarkable
islands, it is not surprising that the great majority of the
birds which frequent them belong to what may be termed
the sea-fowl proper.   Cormorants, gulls, puffins, and guillemots compose by far the greater portion of the countless flocks which resort thither in the breeding season,
and even furnish the chief resident species which in
smaller numbers are to be met with throughout the
year.

GRACULUS BICRISTATUS (Pall.).—The Red-faced Cormorant is said to swarm upon the islands, and remains
there all the year round.   When the gales of February
and March drive other species southward to the open
water, this bird, true to its island home, betakes itself to
the crannies and crevices of the rocks, or rides out the
storm under shelter of the lofty cliffs.   It is a bold and
inquisitive bird, flying round again and again to satisfy
its curiosity, but never alighting on a boat or ship, though
coming close enough sometimes to be almost touched by
the hand.   It is one of the earliest birds to breed, laying

about the first of June, or three weeks in advance of the other seafowl. The nest, composed of sea-ferns (*Sertularie*), grass, &c., is large, carefully rounded, and generally built upon some jutting point or narrow shelf upon the face of a cliff. The eggs, usually three, sometimes four in number, are small for the size of the bird, and in their white chalky appearance closely resemble those of the European cormorant. The young are hatched in three weeks, and are at first almost bare even of down. In six weeks more they are able to fly, and are then nearly as large as their parents ; but it is not until the beginning of the second year that they acquire the bright plumage and metallic gloss of the adult, wearing during the first year a dull drab-brown coat, and having the colours of the base of the bill and gular sac much subdued.

As these birds are found during the whole winter, in spite of severe weather, perched on the sheltered bluffs, the natives regard them with a species of affection, for at that season they furnish the only available supply of fresh meat. When winter has passed, however, and other birds return to the islands, the cormorants are left unmolested.

DIOMEDEA BRACHYURA (Temm.).—Twenty or thirty years ago, when whaling vessels were reaping their rich harvests in Behring and the Arctic seas, the Short-tailed Albatross was often seen about the islands, feeding upon the whale carrion which might drift on shore ; but with the decrease of the whale fishery these birds have almost disappeared. Only a single individual was noted by Mr. Elliott during his two years' residence ; this was taken by Dr. Meany on the north shore of St. George's. Mr. Elliott states that it is common around Ounalaska Island, where he saw a large number on his way to San Francisco in August, 1873.

FULMARUS GLACIALIS (Linn.).—This is the only petrel to be seen on or about the Prybilov Islands. It repairs to the cliffs on the south and east shores of St. George's in great numbers, arriving early in the season, and laying a single white egg on a bare ledge of rock, without any

attempt at a nest. The eggs are generally laid during
the first week of June, and large numbers of them are
gathered by the natives for food. The chick when first
hatched is described by Mr. Elliott as "a perfect puff-
ball of white down," gaining its first plumage in about
six weeks. By the end of the season it resembles its
parents in colour, except that it is much darker on the
back and scapulars. According to Dr. Coues, the bird in
question, which he describes as var. *Rodgersi,* is to be
distinguished from the ordinary Fulmar (*F. glacialis,*
Linnæus), "by the restriction of the darker slate-grey
mantle, most of the wing coverts and some of the second-
aries being white."

STERCORARIUS POMATORHINUS (Vieill.) is included in
Mr. Elliott's list as a rare visitor, the single specimen
secured being the only one seen by him on the islands.
It was found on the high mossy uplands, perched in a
listless attitude on a tussock of grass.

STERCORARIUS PARASITICUS (Linn.) — Four or five
examples of this skua were met with on the islands, where
it is regarded as an occasional visitant.

STERCORARIUS BUFFONI (Boie).—Only two of these
birds were seen, and one secured by Mr. Elliott in July,
1872. They were feeding apparently on insects, and upon
a small black berry (*Empetrum nigrum*), which ripens
upon the higher lands.

LARUS GLAUCUS (Brün.)—This large handsome gull
is restricted by choice to Walrus Island, although it sails
over and around all the islands with an easy graceful flight
almost every hour of the day, and late in autumn will
frequently settle down by hundreds on the carcases of the
seals left upon the killing grounds. It breeds upon Walrus
Island, laying its eggs in a neat nest of sea ferns and dry
grass amongst the grassy tussocks in the centre of the
island. The young are hatched in three weeks, and are
at first clothed in a coat of thick pure white down, which
is gradually superseded by a brownish-black and grey
plumage, which is retained until the bird is able to fly. It

is then nearly the size of the parent. This dark coat changes within the next three months to one nearly white, with the lavender-grey back of the adult ; the legs also change from a pale greyish tone to a rich yellow, and the bill passes from a dull brown colour to a bright yellow, with a red spot on the lower mandible. This gull has a loud shrill cry, which from its repetition soon becomes very monotonous, and it utters also at times a low chattering croak. When Mr. Elliott visited Walrus Island in 1872, there were about five or six hundred nests there.

LARUS TRIDACTYLUS (Linn.).—Under the specific name " *Kotzebui*," the North Pacific Kittiwake has been separated from the Atlantic form, on the ground of its having the hind toe better formed ; but, as Dr. Coues points out, this is the sole basis of the supposed species, and is really too trivial to warrant a specific distinction. In company with *Larus brevirostris*, this kittiwake breeds on the islands "by tens of thousands." The two species arrive much about the same time ; but *tridactylus* lays a week or ten days earlier than *brevirostris* and uses more grass and less mud in the construction of its nest. Its eggs also are more pointed at the smaller end, and lighter in the ground colour, with numerous spots and blotches of dark brown. The chick is difficult to distinguish with certainty from that of *brevirostris*, and it is not until two or three weeks have passed that any difference can be noted in the length of bill and colour of the feet.

LARUS BREVIROSTRIS (Brandt) may be at once distinguished from the last named by its short bill and red legs, the latter in preserved skins drying a straw-yellow colour. It is found upon these islands in equally large numbers with the preceding, and is especially abundant on St. George's Island. Like *Larus glaucus*, it remains about the islands the whole season, coming to the cliffs to breed by the 9th of May, and leaving them when the young are ready for flight early in October. This bird is very constant in its specific characters, but Mr. Elliott has seen a variety in which the feet are nearly yellow, or rather yellow than red, and the eyelids black instead of scarlet, with a dark patch also behind each eye. The colour of the feet, he thinks, is probably an accidental individual peculiarity; the dark eye-patch and absence of bright colour from the eyelids may depend upon season.

COLYMBUS ARCTICUS (Linn.).—A fine Black-throated Diver was found dead upon the beach at Zapadnee, St. George's Island, and brought to Mr. Elliott by the natives. As they differed amongst themselves as to whether they had ever seen the bird before, it must be at all events of rare occurrence there. It is interesting to note that this, the only specimen obtained, is the true *arcticus*, and not *pacificus*, as might have been supposed.

PODICEPS GRISEIGENA (Bodd.).—A single specimen of the Red-necked Grebe was obtained by Mr. Elliott, and was the only one seen by him. The natives had observed the species before, but considered it very uncommon.

FRATERCULA CORNICULATA (Brandt).—The Horned Puffin arrives upon the islands from the south about the 10th of May, in company with the Tufted Puffin, next to be noticed, and travels in pairs, never coming or going in flocks. It does not come in large numbers to the islands, for it breeds everywhere else in Behring Sea. Its flight is performed with quick and rapid wing-beats in a straight and steady course. Mr. Elliott states that no difference is observable between the sexes, either in size or colour. The Horned Puffin makes a nest of dried sea ferns, grass, and moss, placed far back or down in some deep rocky crevice, where its single white egg is generally inaccessible.

FRATERCULA CIRRHATA (Pall.).—The Tufted Puffin arrives on the islands about the same time as the last-named species, and resembles it in habits generally.

PHALERIS PSITTACULA (Pall.).—The Parrot-billed Auk is very common on the Prybilov Islands in the breeding season, and is especially numerous on St. George's. It arrives early in May, and occupies the crevices and fissures of the rocks, wherein it lays a single white egg on the bare ground. It leaves the islands again during the last week of August, and goes out upon the North Pacific for the winter, where it lives upon fish fry and sea fleas (*Amphipoda*). According to Professor Brandt, this bird uses its quaintly-shaped bill for opening mussels and other mollusks, upon which it feeds; but Mr. Elliott states that, amongst the thousands which he had an opportunity of observing upon these islands, he never saw one so employed.

PHALERIS CRISTATELLUS (Pall.).—The Crested Auk, which is conspicuous by its curling crest and bright crimson bill, arrives in May like the last-named, and selects the most inaccessible crevices in the rocks wherein to deposit its single white egg. So difficult is it to get the eggs of this bird, that, after making above a hundred attempts, Mr. Elliott only succeeded in getting four unbroken specimens.

PHALERIS PUSILLA (Pall.).—The Little Horned Auk, identified with *Phaleris microceros*, Brandt, and *nodirostra*, Bonaparte, is one of the most characteristic of the waterfowl frequenting the Prybilov Islands, where it resorts for the purpose of breeding every summer. Mr. Elliott says these little birds arrived "in millions." They frequent the loose stony reefs and boulder bars on St. Paul's, together with the cliffs on both islands, and an area of over five square miles of basaltic shingle on St. George's. They make no nests, but lay a single egg each far down under loose rocks and boulders, whence it is extremely difficult to extract them. A walk over the breeding grounds at this season is most amusing, as the noise of hundreds of these little birds directly under foot gives rise to an endless variation of sound, as it comes up from the stony holes and caverns below; while the birds come and go, in and out, with bewildering rapidity, comically blinking and fluttering. In the morning they go out to sea, where they feed on small water shrimps and sea fleas (*Amphipoda*), returning to their holes in the evening.

LOMVIA TROILE (var. *californica*).—Under this name Dr. Coues describes the Common Guillemot which is found upon the Prybilov Islands amongst very much larger numbers of the Thick-billed Guillemot (*Lomvia arra* vel *Brünnichii*), next to be noticed. He points out how this variety may be always distinguished from the Atlantic *troile* by the peculiar shape of the bill, of which an engraving is given. Mr. Elliott states that, although he has seen as many as fifty of these birds together at one time, they are generally scattered by twos and threes amongst thousands of the Thick-billed Guillemot.

LOMVIA ARRA (Pall.).—This is the great Egg-bird of the North Pacific, and frequents the Prybilov Islands by millions. It arrives in flocks very early in the season, but does not commence laying until the middle of June. The natives assert that in open, mild winters these birds may be seen in straggling flocks all round the islands, and Mr. Elliott feels assured that they do not all migrate from Behring Sea and the vicinity of the Aleutian Islands. They lay each a single egg upon the bare ledges of the rocks, without any nest, and crowd side by side in hundreds and thousands. They quarrel desperately, and hundreds of dead birds may be seen lying on the beach under the high cliffs on the north shore of St. George's, having fallen from above while locked together in mortal conflict. While the females are sitting, about the end of June and beginning of July, the males fly round the island in great files and platoons, always circling against or quartering on the wind, at regular hours in the morning and evening, making a dark girdle of birds more than a quarter of a mile broad and thirty miles long, whirling round and round the island, and forcing upon the most casual observer an extraordinary and lasting impression. To the inhabitants of these islands the Thick-billed Guillemot is a most valuable bird, furnishing them for many months with an enormous supply of eggs and fresh meat.

This species completes the list of birds which have been met with on these islands.

REPTILIA AND PISCES.

No Reptiles were discovered by Mr. Elliott, and only a small list of Fishes rewarded the most careful search. The presence of the Seals in the water about the islands in such great numbers during five and six months of every year renders all kinds of fishing trips abortive, with one exception, made within a radius of at least five miles from land ; and after these animals leave in November and December up to the time of their re-appearance in May and June, the weather is usually too stormy or cold for the fishermen of the islands, who venture out, however, during July and August in their small " kyacks " or " bidarkies " to get the halibut, and meet with some success, catching this bottom fish in fifteen to twenty fathoms of water. They frequently find in its maw several species of octopus and crabs.

ARTICULATA, MOLLUSCA, AND RADIATA.

The Insect world, represented by a large flesh-fly (*Musca*), appears in a very striking manner upon the rank luxuriant masses of sedge-grass which flourish on the killing grounds, springing up in the growing season with almost magical rapidity. This fly is covered with a bluish-grey down, and is very quiet and inoffensive, seldom or never getting into the houses. It settles upon the long grass stems and leaf-blades by millions, causing the verdure over the whole slaughtering district and vicinity to fairly droop to earth with its burden of insect weight ; and at a slight distance the field looks as though a shower of paste had been thrown upon it and had become very mouldy. A gnat (*Culex*) flits about, taking shelter in the grass, but never annoys man, so that virtually there are no mosquitoes on the islands. The common house-fly is never seen upon the islands, not even in the dwellings.

The *Annulosa* are represented by great numbers of *Errantia* or sand worms, and in quiet eddies the *Crustacea* by large swarms of water fleas, *Cypris*, and *Daphnia*. A fine crab is at certain seasons exceedingly abundant, and excellent for the table, and a small hermit crab (*Pagurus*) is found in the empty whelk shells at the tide margin. Numbers of *Amphipoda* or sea fleas of various kinds are also met with.

Several species of *Echinoidea* or sea urchins, and many of the *Scolecidæ* are met with. The natives make a regular search for the sea urchins in fair weather, esteeming them highly as an article of food. The sea is filled with hydroids—a large variety of *Actinia*, or sea anemone, and *Discophora*, or jelly-fish, which, at certain times of the year, and after heavy gales, lie rotting by millions upon the rocks and beaches, where they have been thrown up by the surf. The protozoic classes of *Rhizopoda* and *Infusoria* fairly swarm in the waters about these islands.

In connection with these minute denizens of the sea, the authors remark that forests of *Algæ* are found in every nook and corner which it covers; and a terrestrial species, a silky-green *Conferva*, flourishes over the decaying vegetable and animal matter on the killing grounds of the sealers. All three divisions in this great order—*Melanospermæ*, *Rhodospermæ*, and *Chlorospermæ*—are present, the first-named being, however, the most abundant; and upon decaying heaps of it countless numbers of a common buccinoid, or whelk, feed by boring or sucking out myriads of tiny holes in the leaf fronds.

Woodfall & Kinder, Printers, Milford Lane, Strand, London, W.C.

.

www.ingramcontent.com/pod-product-compliance
Lightning Source LLC
Chambersburg PA
CBHW032142080426
42733CB00008B/1171